Can I tell you about Adoption?

by the same author

The Mulberry Bird
An Adoption Story
Illustrated by Angela Marchetti
ISBN 978 1 84905 933 6
eISBN 978 0 85700 720 9

of related interest

Adopted Like Me
My Book of Adopted Heroes
Ann Angel
Illustrated by Marc Thomas
ISBN 978 1 84905 935 0
eISBN 978 0 85700 740 7

A Safe Place for Caleb
An Interactive Book for Kids, Teens and Adults with Issues of
Attachment, Grief, Loss or Early Trauma
Kathleen A. Chara and Paul J. Chara Jr.
ISBN 978 1 84310 799 6
eISBN 978 1 84642 143 3

Can I tell you about...?

The "Can I tell you about...?" series offers simple introductions to a range of topics and limiting conditions. Friendly characters invite readers to learn about their lives and how they would like to be helped and supported. These books serve as excellent starting points for family and classroom discussions.

other subjects covered in the Can I tell you about...? series
ADHD, Asperger Syndrome, Asthma, Dementia, Dyslexia, Epilepsy, OCD, Parkinson's Disease, Selective Mutism, Stuttering/Stammering

Can I tell you about Adoption?

A guide for friends, family and professionals

ANNE BRAFF BRODZINSKY
Illustrated by Rosy Salaman

Jessica Kingsley *Publishers*
London and Philadelphia

First published in 2013
by Jessica Kingsley Publishers
73 Collier Street
London N1 9BE, UK
and
400 Market Street, Suite 400
Philadelphia, PA 19106, USA

www.jkp.com

Library of Congress Cataloging in Publication Data
Brodzinsky, Anne Braff, 1940-
Can I tell you about adoption? : a guide for friends, family
and professionals / Anne Braff Brodzinsky ;
illustrated by Rosy Salaman.
pages cm
Includes bibliographical references.
Audience: Grade K to 3.
ISBN 978-1-84905-942-8
1. Adopted children--Juvenile literature. 2. Adoption--
Juvenile literature. I. Salaman, Rosy, illustrator.
II. Title.
HV875.B737 2013
362.7340973--dc23
2013023657

British Library Cataloguing in Publication Data
A CIP catalogue record for this book is available from the British Library

ISBN 9781849059428
eISBN 9780857007599

Printed and bound in Great Britain by Bell & Bain Ltd, Glasgow

Contents

Acknowledgements

I would like to acknowledge Stephen Jones at Jessica Kingsley for his editing skills and kind assistance.

I have been assisted in writing this narrative by L. H., A. R. and H. P; all children who have been adopted and are about the age of the children represented in this book.

I would like to thank my graddaughter, Ella, for her thoughtful comments during the final edits of this book.

Introduction

This book has been written to help everyone understand adoption and what it's like to be adopted.

Children and young people reading about both the difficulties and satisfactions experienced by a child who is adopted will have a chance to learn what adoption is, what it feels like to be adopted and how they can help.

It is a useful, friendly book to share with adopted children to help them to understand and talk about how it affects them. It may also help older children who are adopted to talk about their past or present experiences.

And, of course, adults can learn about adoption too!

Extra sections at the back give tips on how parents and teachers can help children who are adopted. All children are different, and all adoptions are different, but the ideas in this book can be adapted to suit different people in all kinds of adoptive families.

"Ten years ago I was adopted."

"Ten years ago I was adopted. Adoption is pretty complicated and kids and adults think they understand it, but actually, a lot of the time, they don't.

I want to try to tell you what I understand about it and what it's like to have been adopted. I want to do this because it would help me if more kids knew about the adoption part of my life.

The way I think about it is, if you knew more about my adoption story, you would understand me better and you would also know more about other kids who have been adopted.

If you have been adopted too, this book might help you to think of questions for your parents and also different ways to talk about adoption to your friends."

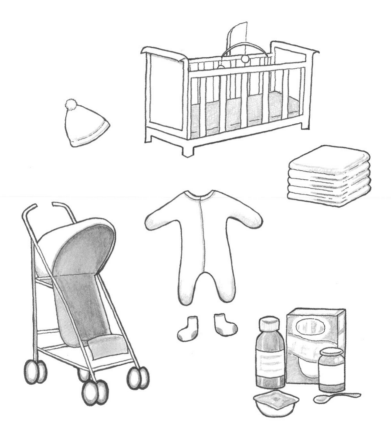

"They fix up a place for the baby
to sleep; they buy a pushchair and
baby clothes. They also buy nappies,
food and medicine for the baby."

"Most of the time when a baby is ready to be born the baby's parents begin to do all the regular things they need to do in order to keep their baby safe and well. They go to a mother and baby doctor so that the doctor can listen to the baby's heart and check up on the mum's health. They fix up a place for the baby to sleep; they buy a pushchair and baby clothes. They also buy nappies, food and medicine for the baby.

Something else happens when a baby is ready to be born. The baby's parents have to get themselves ready to be the ones who will be there every minute for the baby.

That means they will not have the same life that they had before they had a baby. It means they will have to be strong and healthy and brave pretty much all the time. That is what being a parent is like. That is what little babies need their parents to do for them. If their parents can't do that for them, babies can feel afraid and sad and even get sick.

When a baby's parents are not able to do most of the things a baby needs, it is a very serious problem. To understand adoption, you have to understand some things about this kind of problem."

"Every mother knows she must be able to focus a lot of her attention on her child in order to look after the child properly. All mothers worry about this a little bit before their baby is born"

"Let's start at the beginning. All babies begin their life with their own first mother who holds them in her body for nine months. As the time for the birth grows closer and her body grows larger, she has stronger and stronger feelings of love for the baby growing inside her. She thinks a lot about being a mother and wonders if she is going to be able to do all the hard work that will be needed. Every mother knows she must be able to focus a lot of her attention on her child in order to look after the child properly. All mothers worry about this a little bit before their baby is born.

Because being able to focus on a new baby is so important, most new mothers start out trying hard to do all the things their baby needs.

Sometimes even though a mother wants very much to do the right things, she finds that she is not able to. She finds that she is not as strong and brave as she needs to be to keep her baby safe.

It is very hard for a mother to admit this problem to herself and so sometimes she pretends everything is fine. She does this because she is hoping things will change so that she will be able to do a better job."

"You must be wondering why a person might not be able to be a mother to a baby. This is the part of adoption that is the most difficult for *everyone* to figure out. Here is how I understand it.

You see, in order to be a mother, two important things have to happen. The first one is you have to learn how to do it from your own mother, and the second is you have to be healthy in your mind and your body.

If your own mother didn't teach you about love and care of others it can be very hard to be strong and brave and healthy in your mind and your body. So if your mother hasn't taught you these things and you have your own baby, you might want very much to be a mother and be quite sure you could be a mother, but it will be very, very hard for you to do it. Mothers who haven't had a loving mother often make mistakes when they become a parent. Those mistakes are not made on purpose, but they can be dangerous for little babies."

"You might have two parents and be wondering why a mother would be alone with her baby. You might be saying, 'Where is the baby's other parent?' The answer to that is sometimes a baby's father doesn't help the mother. Sometimes he goes away and leaves her alone.

Some of the problems that happen for the baby might be because he left the mother alone and she couldn't do the job alone. Sometimes he stays and causes some of the problems himself.

If a mother is making mistakes in the way she takes care of her baby, even though she is sorry and sad about it (and she always is), and even though she may pretend everything is fine, people around her can usually tell her baby isn't safe. When people find out a baby isn't safe they can call a person called a social worker who will come and visit the family.

Sometimes after the social worker spends some time with the mother and baby, she decides that a safer home needs to be found for the baby. She is kind to the mother and tells her that the baby needs to live with another family until she learns some important things about being a mother. And until she feels strong and brave again."

"In the foster home there are grown-ups who love babies and know how to provide everything they need."

"This kind of home is called a foster home. In the foster home there are grown-ups who love babies and know how to provide everything they need.

A foster home can be the baby's home until the mother is able to take care of the baby, but if the mother cannot find a way to learn to do that, it can be the baby's home until other parents come along and say they will be the baby's parents.

When new parents come and promise to take care of a baby who has been in a foster home, they bring the baby into their family to be their child forever and that is called *adoption*.

An adopted baby's first mother is called the birthmother. It is important to know that birthmothers miss their babies very much and before the baby is adopted they often try very hard to get well and strong so that they can have their baby back. Sometimes they do get their babies back and sometimes they don't."

"My adoptive parents are my family now."

"I was born like everybody else. My parents have told me that my birthmother had an illness that caused her to make a lot of mistakes as a new mother. She loved me and tried hard to do the right things for me, but after a while I had to go and live in a foster home. My foster parents were kind and my adoptive parents say I loved them a lot. It was confusing for me to have to leave them when I was adopted. I got used to my new home, though, and I have been happy with my adoptive parents. My adoptive parents are my family now.

One of the most important things about being adopted is that even though you love your adoptive family, and even though you may be very happy with them, you always keep your birthmother in your mind.

Sometimes my birthmother is kind of in the back of my mind and sometimes she is right up in front. I think about her on my birthday and even though I don't know her, or know where she is, my mum says she is pretty sure she thinks about me on that day too."

"My adoptive parents have made
a book for me about my life."

"My adoptive parents have made a book for me about my life. It is called a Lifebook. The book tells the story of everything that has happened to me since I was born. It tells the story of my birthmother and how hard she tried to take care of me. It has some pictures of my foster parents and other kids who lived with me in their home. And it tells the story of coming to live with my adoptive parents and the home that is my forever home.

My Lifebook is also a place where I write my thoughts about lots of things. I write about adoption, and my friends and my family. I can write to my birthmother too. Even though I know she won't be able to read the letters, it makes me feel closer to her to tell her my thoughts.

Another thing I like to do in my Lifebook is to draw pictures. I do self-portraits and also pictures of things that I imagine.

My mum likes to write in my Lifebook too. She puts important papers about my adoption in there and every year on my birthday she writes a special letter to me and my birthmother. I always like reading that letter. It makes me feel as though we are all a family together."

"I have two friends who were adopted
from different places in the world.
My friend Adilu was born in Ethiopia,
which is a country in Africa. My
friend Kira was born in China."

"I have two friends who were adopted from different places in the world. My friend Adilu was born in Ethiopia, which is a country in Africa. My friend Kira was born in China.

They both lived in orphanages for a couple of years before they were adopted. An orphanage is kind of like a foster home, but instead of there being a few kids living there, there are a lot. There might even be a hundred! Because there are so many kids in an orphanage, there are a lot of grown-ups who take care of them. Some orphanages take really good care of children, but some orphanages do not. Sometimes there are not enough grown-ups to care for the children. Sometimes there isn't enough food for the kids to eat.

Adoption has been happening since people started living together in communities. It is one of the oldest social customs that is known about. What that means now is that in every country in the whole world there are mothers who need someone to adopt their children and in every country in the world there are parents who want to adopt children.

Putting birthmothers and adoptive parents together is complicated and it is a serious responsibility for the people who do it. Probably the most serious part is making sure that the birthmother and her family are absolutely sure they cannot raise the child themselves."

"Before you are adopted you have been on a journey with a lot of different people and a lot of different things happen to you and around you. On this journey many things happen to your birth family, your foster family, the people who took care of you in the orphanage and your adoptive parents too. When you have been adopted all these people have been in your life. You might remember them and you might not, but they will always be part of your life and who you are as a person.

You can't tell I have been adopted just by looking at me because I am white like my adoptive parents, but some adopted kids have brown or yellow skin, or their eyes or hair might be different from their parents. You could make a guess that those kids are adopted and you might be right. Some of them come from other countries far away and some of them are born in our own country.

Adilu and Kira tell me that because they were adopted and look different from their parents, people are always asking them weird questions. That happens to me too! The weird questions can make us feel uncomfortable and even sad. Here are some examples of what I mean:"

"These questions make us feel different and no one likes to feel different."

"We don't like it when people say these things. We don't know how to answer. These questions make us feel different and no one likes to feel different.

If you are curious about a person's adoption story, here are some things you could say:"

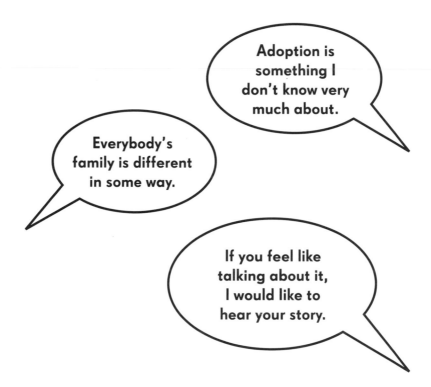

Adoption is something I don't know very much about.

Everybody's family is different in some way.

If you feel like talking about it, I would like to hear your story.

"My friends and I think that it is hard to talk about adoption to other people because when you have been adopted you sometimes have some mysteries or unanswered questions in your life story. You know, it's kind of hard to explain things to other people that you really don't understand very well yourself.

Adilu, Kira and I have a few adoption mysteries and unanswered questions. We wonder about our birthmothers, whether we have brothers and sisters we don't know and we are really curious about the reasons we had to be placed for adoption."

"Adilu, Kira and I have a few adoption mysteries and unanswered questions."

"We wonder about the reasons that we weren't kept by our birthmothers. Sometimes we worry there was something about us that she didn't like.

We don't always tell our adoptive parents the things we are worried about because we think they might not like what we are thinking and feeling...that our thoughts or feelings might make them angry or sad or disappointed.

Another reason that it is hard to answer other kids' questions and talk with our parents about our feelings is that even though adoption has a lot of good parts, it also has some really sad parts.

We are sad that our birthmothers and birthfathers couldn't keep us and take care of us."

"We are sad that we are far away from the places where we were born."

"We are sad that we are far away from the places where we were born. Adilu and Kira are sad that they don't speak the languages their birthparents speak. It is really hard to talk about these feelings.

When you are sad about something it feels kind of private. Even if you have not been adopted you know what that feels like. Even if you are not adopted, you might have some complications and mysteries in your life. Thinking about those things might help you to understand how it feels to have been adopted."

"There are some other things that are hard about adoption. Kids who have been in foster homes and orphanages remember adults that they loved who were like parents to them in those homes. They also had friends there – other kids who lived there and were part of their family. Sometimes foster children even get separated from their brothers and sisters who might have been in the foster home or orphanage with them. When they were adopted, no one seemed to understand that it was hard to say goodbye to those people. Also, some of the grown-ups in those early homes were not good to them. Some kids have those memories too.

So, let's go back to that list of difficult questions. There are a lot of them, but on the next pages you will see two of the hardest ones to answer."

"How come she didn't want you?"

"A birthmother almost always WANTS her baby. All babies are sweet and soft and cuddly and they smell really good. They don't have things about them people don't like. But, you might be saying, what kind of problem could be so serious that a mother would have to ask another person to take care of her baby?

Some of those serious problems are:

- She is really, really poor and has no home or money to buy things for the baby.

- She can't keep the baby safe.

- The baby's father has left her alone.

- She asks family and friends to help her, but none of them can or will do it.

- She has an illness that isn't going to get better.

- She has an illness that makes her weak and tired and causes her to make mistakes.

- She is too young to be a mother.

A birthmother may just have one of these problems, or she may have more than one."

"Sometimes birthmothers and their children who have been adopted do hear from each other again."

**"Do you think you will ever
see your birthmother again?"**

"Sometimes birthmothers and their children who have been adopted do hear from each other again. When this happens it is called 'open adoption'. If they live far apart they might be able to write letters to each other. If they live closer they might be able to visit. When birth families live in another country, like China, it is very hard and very unusual to have an open adoption.

Sometimes when adopted children grow up to be adults they search for their birthmother and their birthfather. Sometimes birthmothers and birthfathers search for their child that was adopted. Some of these searches are successful and some are not. Most people who have been adopted think about searching for and finding their birthparents."

"Now that I have told you a lot of serious and sad things about adoption, it's time to smile! The reason for smiling is that adoption has so many great things about it!"

"Now that I have told you a lot of serious and sad things about adoption, it's time to smile! The reason for smiling is that adoption has so many great things about it!

First of all you have a forever family that loves you and thinks you are the greatest! You love them too of course and you love being there with them in the circle of the family.

Our family has some really fun rituals we look forward to every year. Some of them are about holidays, but some of them are just the silly stuff only we know about.

We go to the seaside and to the zoo and to Grandma and Grandpa for Sunday dinner. We have an amazing dog named Charlie and we might get some fish.

My mum and dad listen to me and we make lists of things we like and things we would like to change. We share our lists and laugh a lot too.

As you get older you understand more and more about your adoption. Each year my parents tell me more about my early life – they promise me that as I get older they will tell me even more until when I am grown up I will know everything they know.

Adoptive families are not perfect, but nobody's family is perfect. We are a lot like other families, but we have a special story about how we found each other.

The experience of being adopted helps me to understand that other kids have complicated things in their lives too. It makes me remember to be kind."

"So now that you know some basic facts about adoption, Adilu and Kira and I want you to be our *ambassador*."

"So now that you know some basic facts about adoption, Adilu and Kira and I want you to be our *ambassador*. An ambassador is someone who stands up for another person or place. They go out into the world and spread the word. They do this proudly and they use all the things they have learned to let others know about what they stand for. Can you stand up for adoption?

You have learned that ever since the world began there have been kids who start out with one family and end up with another. You have learned that in between their two families they sometimes live in orphanages or foster families. You have learned that the journey before an adoption can be difficult, but sometimes there are people to love along the way.

I hope you have learned that adopted kids sometimes hear questions from other kids that upset them and that there are some really good things to say when you are curious about somebody's adoption.

Finally, remember that adoptive families are a lot like your family and your friends' families. We have a lot of fun and we love each other a lot.

Conclusion! I'm not crazy about that word. Sounds like 'Wrap it up... Time to go home... End of story!' I feel as though I am just getting started. I want to keep talking with you about these important things – at least they are really important to me. But I will say goodbye for now and hope that when you next meet an adopted friend you will remember me, Chelsea. I am adopted. I am counting on you."

How parents can help

A lot has been written about the emotional needs of children who have been adopted but at the core of all these books and articles are a few central issues.

Children long to have parents who know how to leap the tallest buildings and swim the widest seas to reach their secret sadness and their hidden fears. In short, they long to be known by their parents. Adoptive parents come to this task at some risk. Adopting a child is often undertaken as a path to healing their own hurt and loss about being unable to conceive.

This healing path is marked with specific signs that promise a child "We will be your parents. We will take full responsibility. We will love you very deeply. You will not have to worry. We will ease your way in the world." They trust, as does every parent, that this extraordinary love and commitment will be felt and accepted and returned. However, when adopted children reach the approximate age of seven or eight most begin to experience some measure of unrest about their history. Many become curious about what happened in the time before they can remember and will express feelings of loss and longing for their birthmother. The stories they have been told about her and the way the adoption came to be no longer seem adequate. They want to know details about the reasons she was unable to parent, they may want to meet her, they may become preoccupied with the culture they were born to and express disdain for the culture of the adoptive parents. They sometimes tell their adoptive parents that their birthmother is their "real mother". For many adoptive parents, this development is jarring and upsetting. Some have said that it feels like a betrayal. No wonder. The entire situation that exists in the child's mind may run counter to everything that the parents assumed to be true. The healing of their own loss may have been dependent upon the child's acceptance of the adoptive family as their real family – their only real family. In reality, the child has not betrayed them. The child now looks to them and asks to be known in all their confusion and grief. The child needs to be known as they really are in the world. *Can I tell you about Adoption?* is meant to help children express to other children, and their parents, what it is like to have been adopted.

The book has the potential to be a window into the world of the child. The adoptive parents who are able to meet the challenge of facing their child's intense curiosity about the past are likely to find rather than increased distance and betrayal, there is the potential for a new closeness and shared understanding.

Open communication about the reasons for children's placement in foster care, empathy for children's sadness for themselves and for their birthmother and a commitment to discovering new ways of exploring their growing understanding and interest in their birth family will deepen family ties and open the way to a better relationship with the children as adults.

It is essential that adoptive parents have open communication with their children. They need to give sensitive consideration to foster care placements, and their children's sadness for themselves and for their birthmother. They need to be committed to discovering new ways of helping them with their growing understanding of their adoption and interest in their birthfamily. This commitment will deepen family ties and open the way to a better relationship with the child and soon to be adolescent.

How teachers can help

Most universities and colleges preparing young people to be educators do not spend much (if any) time teaching their students about adoption and foster care. This is unfortunate because during your career, most of you will be asked to teach many children who have spent some time in foster care and/or have been adopted. Each one of these children will sit in your classes, go on your field trips, navigate the social situations of every school community and do all these things carrying a set of unique circumstances as part of their reality...a reality that you may know nothing about.

This predicament leaves adoptive parents with a dilemma. Many worry that if they reveal to the school that their child has been adopted then any difficulty the child might have will be inappropriately attributed to the adoption. If they do not reveal that the child has been adopted, and circumstances arise that prove confusing or upsetting to the child, there will be no one there who understands or can let the parents know that there has been a problem.

Consider a common example. A teacher announces to her nine-year-old pupils that she is giving them a special assignment. They are to construct a family tree. She shows them an example and explains that the people on their family tree are people who are *related* to them. If she stops there, children who no longer live with their biological family may feel confused and uncomfortable. However, a teacher giving instructions on how to create a family tree can easily say instead that there are many ways in which families differ from each other and give some examples including blended families, adoptive families, foster families and families where someone important may have died. She can go on to say that everyone important to you can be on your family tree, even if you haven't seen them in a long time.

Adoptive parents often say that they prefer to be told in advance about the family tree assignment. This way they can let their child's teacher know how they would like the issue handled and they can be prepared to support their child in the ways they think best.

A more subtle example may occur when the class is studying the history of their country's development and the teacher describes the ways in which people overcame terrible hardship in order to keep their families together, or a novel is read where a mother goes to extreme ends to save her baby from starvation and danger.

In an internationally diverse school where the author works as a consultant, birthdays are celebrated by having the parents and the child walk around a globe and stop next to the country where the child was born. Internationally adopting parents and their children are invited to teach the class an interesting fact about the country where the child was born. This custom could be developed to include different geographical areas such as different countries or regions of the UK or different states in the US. Food and music typical of the area can be shared. These inclusive rituals are educational and heartwarming for all.

As a teacher of young children remember to be curious about how your assignments may impact various children in your care. Most adoptive parents are eager to consult with you and will offer their time generously when invited. Most communities have adoption and foster care professionals with whom to consult. Ask for in-service training or programmes focused on family diversity. There are many ways to facilitate your own education and that of your colleagues, about adoption. The foster and adopted children that you will come to know throughout your career will be grateful for your efforts.

Recommended reading, resources and organisations

BOOKS FOR PARENTS

Brodzinsky, D. M., Schechter, M. D. and Henig, R. M. (1992) *Being Adopted: The Lifelong Search for Self*. New York: Doubleday.

Eldridge, S. (1999) *Twenty Things Adopted Kids Wish Their Parents Knew*. New York: Random House.

James, A. (2013) *Welcoming a New Brother or Sister Through Adoption*. London and Philadelphia, PA: Jessica Kingsley Publishers.

Lifton, B. J. (1994) *Journey of the Adopted Self: A Quest for Wholeness*. New York: Basic Books.

MacLeod, J. and Macrae, S. (eds) (2006) *Adoptive Parenting: Creating a Tool Box, Building Connections*. Warren, NJ: EMK Press.

Pavao, J. M. (1998) *The Family of Adoption*. Boston, MA: Beacon Press.

Pertman, A. (2011) *Adoption Nation: How the Adoption Revolution Has Transformed America*. Boston, MA: The Harvard Common Press.

Steinberg, G. and Hall, B. (2013) *Inside Transracial Adoption* (second edition). London and Philadelphia, PA: Jessica Kingsley Publishers.

BOOKS FOR TEACHERS

Meese, R. L. (2002) *Children of Intercountry Adoptions in School: A Primer for Parents and Professionals.* Westport, CT: Bergin & Garvey Publishing Group.

BOOKS FOR CHILDREN 5–12

Brodzinsky, A. B. (2013) *The Mulberry Bird.* London and Philadelphia, PA: Jessica Kingsley Publishers.

Christian, D. R. (2012) *An-Ya and Her Diary.* United Kingdom: Shoofly Press.

Curtis, C. P. (1999) *Bud, Not Buddy.* New York: Random House Children's Books, Yearling.

Kremetz, J. (2009) *How It Feels to be Adopted.* New York: Alfred Knopf.

Lifton, B. J. (1984) *Tell Me a Real Adoption Story.* New York: Alfred Knopf.

Ryan, P. M. (2007) *Becoming Naomi Leon.* New York: Scholastic Inc.

BOOKS FOR BIRTHPARENTS

Foge, L. (2012) *The Third Choice: A Woman's Guide to Placing a Child for Adoption* (second edition). Self Published: Amazon.

Pedley, J. (2010) *Secrets to Your Successful Domestic Adoption.* Deerfield Beach, FL: Health Communications Inc.

DVDS

Living on the Fault Line: Where Race and Family Meet, Jeff Farber, 2009, available at www.onthefaultline.com.

Adopted, Barb Lee, 2008, available at www.adoptedthemovie.com.

Struggle for Identity: Issues in Transracial Adoption, Deborah C. Hoard, 2007, available at nysccc.org/about-us/programs/ nysccc-videos/struggle-for-identity.

Off and Running: An American Coming of Age Story, Nicole Opper, 2009, available at offandrunningthefilm.com.

ORGANISATIONS AND WEBSITES
UK
BAAF (British Association for Adoption and Fostering)
Saffron House
6–10 Kirby Street
London
EC1N 8TS
Phone: 020 7421 2600
Email: mail@baaf.org.uk
Website: www.baaf.org.uk

Adoption UK
Linden House
55 The Green
South Bar Street
Banbury
OX16 9AB
Phone: 01295 752240
Website: www.adoptionuk.org

Family Futures Consortium Ltd
3–4 Floral Place
7–9 Northampton Grove
Islington
London
N1 2PL
Phone: 020 7354 4161
Email: contact@familyfutures.co.uk
Website: www.familyfutures.co.uk

Adoptionplus
Moulsoe Business Centre
Cranfield Road
Moulsoe
Newport Pagnell
MK16 0FJ
Phone: 01908 218251
Email: Enquiries@adoptionplus.co.uk
Website: www.adoptionplus.co.uk

After Adoption
Unit 5 Citygate
5 Blantyre Street
Manchester
M15 4JJ
Phone: 0161 839 4932
Email: information@afteradoption.org.uk
Website: www.afteradoption.org.uk

Post Adoption Centre (PAC)
5 Torriano Mews
London
NW5 2RZ
Phone: 020 7284 0555
Email: enquiries@pac.org.uk
Website: www.pac.org.uk

USA

Adoptive Families
39 West 37th Street, 15th Floor
New York, NY 10018
www.adoptivefamilies.com
Phone: (800) 372 3300

ARIS (Adoption Referral and Information Service)
Yolanda Comparan, MSW
www.adoptionreferralservice.com
Phone: (888) 777 1538

ATTACh, Association for Treatment and Training in the Attachment of Children
PO Box 19122
Minneapolis, MN 55419
www.attach.org
Email: questions@attach.org
Phone: (612) 866 5499

CASE Center for Adoption Support and Education
4000 Blackburn Lane, Suite 260
Burtonsville, MD 20866
http://adoptionsupport.org
Phone: (301) 476 8525

ChildTrauma Academy
5161 San Felipe, Suite 320
Houston, TX 77056
www.childtrauma.org
Email: cta@childtrauma.org
Phone: (866) 943 9779

Child Information Gateway
Children's Bureau/ACYF
1250 Maryland Avenue, SW
Eighth Floor
Washington, DC 20024
www.childwelfare.gov
Email: info@childtrauma.org

Pact, An Adoption Alliance
4179 Piedmont Avenue, Suite 101
Oakland, CA 94611
www.pactadopt.org
Email: info@pactadopt.org
Phone: (510) 243 9460

Canada

Adoption Council of Canada
The Adoption Council of Canada
211 Bronson Avenue
Mailbox #231
Ottawa, Ontario
K1R 6H5
www.adoption.ca
Email: info@adoption.ca
Phone: 1 888 542 3678

Canada Adopts!
www.canadaadopts.com
Email: info@canadaadopts.com

Australia

Fostering and Adoption Services
161 Great Eastern Highway, Belmont WA 6104
Postal address: PO Box 641, Belmont WA 6984
www.childprotection.wa.gov.au
Email: adoptions@dcp.wa.gov.au
Phone: (08) 9259 3414

Australians Caring For Children (ACC)
Address: PO Box 7182, Bondi Beach NSW 2026
www.accau.org
Email: info@accau.org
Phone: (612) 9389 1889

Blank, for your notes